Special Thanks

I would like to extend my deepest gratitude to the following individuals who have contributed to my journey and supported me throughout the creation of this book:

To God, for imparting wisdom and understanding, and guiding me through the writing process.
James 1:5 says, "If any of you lacks wisdom, let him ask of God, who gives to all liberally and without reproach, and it will be given to him"

> To my friends and family, for their unwavering encouragement, love, and support. For their valuable insights, expertise, and contributions to this book. Your input has been invaluable, and I am grateful for your willingness to share your knowledge with me.

1. Christopher Breaux, Board member/ Real Estate Advisor / Director
2. Corey Weiner, Board member / Construction consultant
3. Simon Singh, Board member / Advisor
4. Susana Penalosa, Board member / Advisor
5. David Salter, Advisor
6. Sarka Ondrackova Bockmeulen, Floral Designer / Artist
7. Liehventz Gilles, Advisor
8. Calatrava Slade, Chief editor and research

Thank you all again for your support and contributions. I am honored to have had the opportunity to work with a great team and learn from each of you.

To all the innovative developers and astute financial advisors,

As you continue to shape the built environment and guide investment decisions, remember that the future of our cities and communities depends on your expertise and foresight.

Stay ahead of the curve by embracing sustainable design principles, incorporating cutting-edge technologies, and promoting socially responsible investments.

Together, let's create thriving, resilient, and equitable communities that benefit generations to come.

Best regards!"

The Greatest Re-set, Commercial Real Estate

Part 1: Introduction to Commercial Real Estate
- Chapter 1: Overview of Commercial Real Estate
- Chapter 2: Types of Commercial Properties (office, retail, industrial, multifamily, etc.)
- Chapter 3: Benefits and Risks of Investing in Commercial Real Estate

Part 2: Investing in Commercial Real Estate

- Chapter 4: Understanding Commercial Real Estate Markets
- Chapter 5: Evaluating Commercial Properties for Investment
- Chapter 6: Financing Options for Commercial Real Estate Investments
- Chapter 7: Tax Strategies for Commercial Real Estate Investors

Part 3: Development and Redevelopment

- Chapter 8: Introduction to Commercial Real Estate Development
- Chapter 9: Site Selection and Acquisition
- Chapter 10: Entitlements and Approvals

- Chapter 11: Construction and Project Management
- Chapter 12: Redevelopment and Repositioning of Commercial Properties

Part 4: Property Management and Operations

- Chapter 13: Introduction to Commercial Property Management
- Chapter 14: Leasing and Tenant Relations
- Chapter 15: Property Maintenance and Repairs
- Chapter 16: Financial Management and Accounting for Commercial Properties

Part 5: Advanced Topics and Trends

- Chapter 17: Sustainable and Energy-Efficient Commercial Properties
- Chapter 18: Technology and Innovation in Commercial Real Estate
- Chapter 19: Impact of Economic and Market Trends on Commercial Real Estate
- Chapter 20: Future of Commercial Real Estate: Trends and Opportunities

IMPORTANT DISCLOSURE

Blue Water Holding Group, a Real Estate Investment Trust ("REIT"), is providing this information for informational purposes only. This information is not intended to be, and should not be construed as, investment advice or a solicitation to buy or sell any securities. Investing in commercial real estate, including through a REIT, involves significant risks, including but not limited to:
- Market risks, such as fluctuations in property values and rental income
- Tenant risks, such as vacancy and non-payment of rent
- Financing risks, such as changes in interest rates and availability of debt
- Regulatory risks, such as changes in laws and regulations affecting real estate investments
- Environmental risks, such as contamination and natural disasters

Before making any investment decision, you should consult with a professional, such as an attorney or accountant, who can provide advice tailored to your individual circumstances and goals.

Blue Water Holding Group is not responsible for any losses or damages arising from the use of this information. By using this information, you acknowledge that you understand and agree to these terms.

Foreword: Strategies, Concepts, and Ideas for Success in Commercial Real Estate

As the commercial real estate landscape continues to evolve, investors, developers, and property owners must stay ahead of the curve to succeed. This book provides a comprehensive guide to the strategies, concepts, and ideas that are shaping the commercial real estate industry today.

From the fundamentals of commercial real estate investing to the latest trends and innovations, this book covers it all. You'll learn about the key drivers of commercial real estate value, including location, demographics, and market trends. You'll also discover how to identify and capitalize on opportunities, manage risk, and build a successful commercial real estate portfolio.

Throughout this book, we'll explore the latest strategies and concepts in commercial real estate, including:

- The impact of technology and innovation on commercial real estate

- The growing importance of sustainability and energy efficiency
- The role of data analytics and market research in informed decision-making
- The opportunities and challenges presented by emerging trends and markets

Whether you're a seasoned commercial real estate professional or just starting out, this book provides the insights, ideas, and inspiration you need to succeed in today's fast-paced and competitive market. So let's get started on this journey through the world of commercial real estate!

The Greatest Re-set, Commercial Real Estate

Introduction to Commercial Real Estate

Commercial real estate is a dynamic and complex industry that plays a vital role in shaping the modern landscape. From the towering skyscrapers of metropolitan cities to the bustling retail centers of suburban towns, commercial properties are the backbone of local economies, providing spaces for businesses to thrive, people to work, and communities to grow. Commercial real estate encompasses a broad range of property types, including office buildings, retail centers, industrial parks, multifamily apartments, hotels, and more. Each property type has its unique characteristics, challenges, and opportunities, requiring a deep understanding of the local market, consumer behavior, and economic trends. Investing in commercial real estate can be a lucrative and rewarding experience, offering potential benefits such as rental income, capital appreciation, and tax benefits. However, it also requires careful planning, thorough research, and a solid understanding of the complex factors that influence the commercial real estate market.

Commercial real estate has indeed outperformed the stock market over the past 25 years, making it an attractive option for savvy investors. To become part owners of Real Estate Investment Trusts (REITs), investors can explore various options.

Investing in REITs

REITs allow individuals to invest in a diversified portfolio of properties without directly managing them. By investing in REITs, individuals can earn rental income and benefit from property appreciation [1].

Benefits of Investing in REITs

- Diversification: REITs provide a way to diversify your portfolio by investing in real estate without directly managing properties.
- Income Generation: REITs can provide a steady stream of income through rental properties and other real estate investments.
- Liquidity: REITs are traded on major stock exchanges, providing liquidity for investors.

By investing in REITs, savvy investors can tap into the potential of commercial real estate and diversify their portfolios.

The future of REITs looks promising, with a potential recovery on the horizon. As the Federal Reserve's tightening cycle comes to an end, REITs are well-positioned for outsized performance in 2024 [1]. Historically, REITs have enjoyed strong absolute and relative total return performances after monetary policy tightening cycles end.

Key Trends to Watch:

- Valuation Convergence: The gap between REIT implied and private appraisal-based cap rates is likely to close or converge in 2024, making REITs an attractive option for investors [1].

- Solid Balance Sheets: REITs' well-managed balance sheets will enable them to navigate economic uncertainty in 2024 and provide an advantage in terms of acquisitions and growth [1].

- Real-Time Market Making: Real-time market making for real estate property is becoming increasingly important, with platforms like Real Estate Investment Trusts (REITs) providing a way for individuals to invest in real estate without directly managing properties [2].

Sector Outlook:
- Shopping-Center REITs: Shopping-center REITs, such as SITE Centers and Urban Edge Properties, are expected to perform well in 2025 and the future, driven by strong fundamentals and favorable supply-and-demand dynamics [2].
- Data Centers: Data centers are another area of growth, with big companies like benefiting from the increasing demand for cloud storage and artificial intelligence [2].
- Senior Housing: Senior housing is also expected to perform well, driven by demographic trends and the increasing demand for age-restricted housing [2].
Self-storage REITs are expected to perform well in 2025 to 2030, driven by several factors. Despite facing a mixed picture on the demand front, with some new customer habits formed during the pandemic persisting, the sector is poised for growth [1].

Key Trends to Watch:
- Consolidation: The self-storage industry remains highly fragmented, with REITs owning only about 15% to 20% of storage assets in the US. This presents opportunities for consolidation and growth [1].
- Supply and Demand: While new supply is expected to come online in 2025, REITs are well-positioned to absorb this new supply, particularly in high-growth markets like Texas and Florida [1].
- Modern Facilities: The trend towards modern, high-tech storage facilities is expected to continue, with consumers prioritizing amenities like touchless entry and climate-controlled units [1].

Outlook for 2025:
Analysts expect self-storage REITs to perform well in 2025 to 2030, driven by a combination of factors, including consolidation, growing demand, and the trend towards modern facilities. While there may be some challenges ahead, particularly in terms of new supply, REITs are well-positioned to navigate these challenges and deliver strong performance [1,2].

Summary of the Book

This book provides a comprehensive overview of the commercial real estate industry, covering topics such as the history of commercial real estate, key players in the industry, types of commercial properties, and current trends in the market. We will also explore the different types of commercial properties, including office buildings, retail centers, industrial parks, multifamily apartments, and hotels. Additionally, we will discuss the benefits and drawbacks of investing in commercial real estate, as well as the different types of investments available, including direct property investment, real estate investment trusts (REITs), fractional investing and real estate crowdfunding.

Chapter 1: **Overview of Commercial Real Estate**

Commercial real estate is a vast and complex industry that encompasses a wide range of property types, investment strategies, and career paths. In this chapter, we'll provide an overview of the commercial real estate industry, including its history, key players, and current trends.

1.1 **History of Commercial Real Estate**

The concept of commercial real estate dates back to ancient times, when merchants and traders established marketplaces and trading centers. However, the modern commercial real estate industry began to take shape in the late 19th and early 20th centuries, with the development of office buildings, retail stores, and industrial facilities. The industry experienced significant growth and transformation over the 20th century, driven by advances in technology, changes in consumer behavior, and shifts in the global economy.

1.2 **Key Players in Commercial Real Estate**

The commercial real estate industry involves a diverse range of players, including Investors: Individuals, companies, and institutions that invest in commercial properties for rental income, capital appreciation, or tax benefits.
Developers: Companies and individuals that develop new commercial properties or redevelop existing ones.
Property managers: Companies and individuals responsible for the day-to-day management of commercial properties.
Brokers and agents: Professionals who facilitate transactions between buyers and sellers, landlords and tenants.
Lenders: Banks, mortgage companies, and other financial institutions that provide financing for commercial real estate transactions.

1.3 **Types of Commercial Properties**

Commercial properties can be broadly categorized into several types, including:
Office buildings: Properties used for office space, such as corporate headquarters, medical offices, and co-working spaces.

Retail properties: Properties used for retail sales, such as shopping centers, restaurants, and convenience stores.

Industrial properties: Properties used for industrial purposes, such as manufacturing, warehousing, and logistics.

Multifamily properties: Properties used for residential purposes, such as apartments, condominiums, and townhouses.

Hospitality properties: Properties used for hospitality purposes, such as hotels, motels, and resorts.

Specialized properties: Properties used for specific purposes, such as healthcare facilities, educational institutions, and government buildings.

1.4 **Current Trends in Commercial Real Estate**

The commercial real estate industry is constantly evolving, with new trends and technologies emerging all the time. Some of the current trends in commercial real estate include:

Sustainability and energy efficiency: The increasing demand for environmentally friendly and energy-efficient buildings.
Technology and innovation: The use of technologies such as artificial intelligence, block chain, and the Internet of things (IoT) to improve the efficiency and profitability of commercial properties.
Shift to experiential retail: The growing demand for retail spaces that offer unique and immersive experiences.
Rise of co-working and flexible office space: The increasing popularity of shared office spaces and flexible leasing arrangements.
Increased focus on wellness and amenities: The growing demand for commercial properties that offer amenities and services that promote wellness and productivity.

1.5 **Real Estate Investment Trusts (REITs)**

A Real Estate Investment Trust (REIT) is a type of company that owns or finances income-generating real estate properties, such as office buildings, apartment complexes, shopping centers, and hotels. REITs allow individuals to invest in a diversified portfolio of properties without directly managing them.

Key Characteristics of a REIT:

1. Ownership Structure: A REIT is a company that is owned by shareholders who purchase shares of the company's stock.
2. Income Generation: REIT

Glossary of Key Terms

Here is a list of definitions for key commercial real estate terms:
- Absorption Rate: The rate at which available space is leased or sold in a given market.
- Amortization: The process of gradually paying off a debt, such as a mortgage.
- Appraisal: An independent opinion of the value of a property.
- Broker: A licensed professional who represents buyers, sellers, landlords, or tenants in commercial real estate transactions.
- Cap Rate: The rate of return on a property based on its net operating income.
- Cash Flow: The net income from a property after expenses and debt service.

- Commercial Property: A property used for business purposes, such as office buildings, retail centers, and industrial parks.
- Developer: A company or individual that develops new commercial properties or redevelops existing ones.
- Due Diligence: The process of researching and verifying the details of a property before making a purchase or investment decision.
- Escrow: A third-party account that holds funds or documents until certain conditions are met.
- Investment Property: A property purchased with the intention of generating income or profits through rental, sale, or other means.
- Lease: A contract between a landlord and tenant that outlines the terms and conditions of property use.
- Lender: A financial institution or individual that provides financing for commercial real estate transactions.
- Net Operating Income (NOI): The income generated by a property after operating expenses are deducted.
- Property Management: The process of overseeing and maintaining a property on behalf of its owner.

- Real Estate Investment Trust (REIT): A company that owns or finances income-generating real estate properties and provides a way for individuals to invest in a diversified portfolio of properties.
- Tenant: An individual or company that rents or leases a property from a landlord.

Commercial Real Estate Cycle

The commercial real estate cycle refers to the fluctuations in the market that affect property values, rental rates, and investment returns. The cycle consists of four phases:

1. Expansion: A period of economic growth, low unemployment, and increasing demand for commercial space. During this phase, property values and rental rates tend to rise.
2. Peak: The point at which the market reaches its highest level of activity and prices. At this stage, the market may be considered overvalued, and a correction may be imminent.
3. Contraction: A period of economic decline, high unemployment, and decreasing demand for commercial space. During this phase, property values and rental rates tend to fall.

4. Trough: The point at which the market reaches its lowest level of activity and prices. At this stage, the market may be considered undervalued, and a recovery may be imminent.

Understanding the commercial real estate cycle is essential for investors, developers, and property owners to make informed decisions about buying, selling, and managing commercial properties.

Key Players' Roles and Responsibilities

The commercial real estate industry involves a diverse range of players, each with their own roles and responsibilities:
1. Investors: Individuals, companies, or institutions that invest in commercial properties for rental income, capital appreciation, or tax benefits.
2. Developers: Companies or individuals that develop new commercial properties or redevelop existing ones.

3. Property Managers: Companies or individuals responsible for the day-to-day management of commercial properties, including maintenance, repairs, and tenant relations.
4. Brokers and Agents: Licensed professionals who represent buyers, sellers, landlords, or tenants in commercial real estate transactions.
5. Lenders: Financial institutions or individuals that provide financing for commercial real estate transactions.

Commercial Real Estate Investment Strategies

Commercial real estate investors can employ various strategies to achieve their investment goals:
1. Core Investing: Investing in high-quality, income-generating properties with a low-risk profile.
2. Value-Add Investing: Investing in properties that require renovation, repositioning, or other forms of value enhancement.
3. Opportunistic Investing: Investing in properties that offer high potential returns, but also come with higher risks.

4. Debt Investing: Investing in debt securities, such as mortgages or mezzanine loans, that's backed by commercial properties.

Global Commercial Real Estate Trends

The commercial real estate market is influenced by global trends and factors:
1. Urbanization: The migration of people from rural areas to cities, driving demand for commercial and residential space.
2. E-commerce: The growth of online shopping, changing the way retailers operate and the type of space they require.
3. Sustainability: The increasing focus on environmental sustainability and energy efficiency in commercial properties.
4. Technology: The impact of technological advancements, such as artificial intelligence and the Internet of Things, on commercial real estate operations and investment strategies.
These trends and factors can have significant implications for commercial real estate investors, developers, and property owners.

Chapter 2:

Types of Commercial Properties

Commercial properties can be broadly categorized into several types, each with its unique characteristics, advantages, and challenges. Understanding the different types of commercial properties is essential for investors, developers, and property owners to make informed decisions about buying, selling, and managing commercial properties. In this chapter, we'll explore the main types of commercial properties, including office, retail, industrial, multifamily, and hospitality properties.

2.1 **Office Properties**

Office properties are designed to provide space for businesses, organizations, and professionals to operate. They can range from small, single-tenant buildings to large, multi-tenant skyscrapers. Office properties can be further sub-divided into:

- Central Business District (CBD) Offices: Located in the heart of cities, these offices are often high-rise buildings with high-end finishes and amenities.
- Suburban Offices: Located outside of city centers, these offices are often lower-rise buildings with more parking and easier access.
- Medical Offices: Specialized offices designed for medical professionals, often with specific layouts and equipment requirements.

2.2 **Retail Properties**

Retail properties are designed to provide space for businesses to sell goods and services to consumers. They can range from small, single-tenant stores to large, multi-tenant shopping centers. Retail properties can be further sub-divided into:

- Neighborhood Centers: Small, convenience-oriented shopping centers with a mix of local retailers and services.
- Community Centers: Medium-sized shopping centers with a mix of national and local retailers, liquor stores often with a grocery store anchor.

- Regional Malls: Large, enclosed shopping centers with a mix of national and local retailers, often with department store anchors.
- Power Centers: Large, open-air shopping centers with a mix of big-box retailers and restaurants.
- Convenience Store (C-Store) Properties: These are retail properties that combine a convenience store with a fuel station, often with additional amenities such as a car wash, tire repair, vending machines, restaurant, or ATM.
- Gas Station Properties: These are retail properties that primarily sell fuel, often with a small convenience store or other ancillary services.
- Service Station Properties: These are retail properties that provide a range of services, including fuel sales, car washes, oil changes, and other automotive services.

These types of retail properties can offer stable cash flow through fuel sales and convenience store operations, as well as potential for long-term appreciation in property value. However, they can also come with unique challenges, such as environmental concerns related to fuel storage and handling, regulatory requirements for fuel sales and convenience store operations, and potential for liability related to accidents or other incidents on the property.

2.3 **Industrial Properties**

Industrial properties are designed to provide space for businesses to manufacture, distribute, and store goods. They can range from small, single-tenant warehouses to large, multi-tenant industrial parks. Industrial properties can be further sub-divided into:
- Light Industrial: Small, flexible spaces for businesses that require minimal heavy manufacturing or storage.
- Heavy Industrial: Large, specialized spaces for businesses that require heavy manufacturing, storage, or distribution.

- Warehouse/Distribution: Spaces designed for the storage and distribution of goods, often with high ceilings and dock doors.

2.4 **Multifamily Properties**

Multifamily properties are designed to provide residential space for multiple families or individuals. They can range from small, apartment buildings to large, high-rise complexes. Multifamily properties can be further sub-divided into:
- Garden-Style Apartments: Low-rise, walk-up apartments with direct access to outdoor spaces.
- Mid-Rise Apartments: Medium-rise, elevator-served apartments with a mix of studios, one-, two-, and three-bedroom units.
- High-Rise Apartments: Tall, elevator-served apartments with a mix of studios, one-, two-, and three-bedroom units, often with luxury amenities.

2.5 **Hospitality Properties**

Hospitality properties are designed to provide temporary accommodations for travelers, tourists, and business professionals. They can range from small, boutique hotels to large, luxury resorts. Hospitality properties can be further sub-divided into:

- Limited-Service Hotels: Basic, no-frills hotels with minimal amenities.
- Full-Service Hotels: Mid-range hotels with a mix of amenities, such as restaurants, fitness centers, and meeting spaces.
- Luxury Hotels: High-end hotels with premium amenities, such as spas, fine dining restaurants, and personalized services.

2.6 **Specialized Properties**

Specialized properties are designed to meet specific needs or provide unique services. They can include:

- Healthcare Properties: Medical offices, hospitals, clinics, and other healthcare facilities.

- Education Properties: Schools, universities, and other educational institutions.
- Government Properties: Government offices, courthouses, and other public facilities.
- Data Centers: Specialized facilities designed to store and process large amounts of data.

In conclusion, commercial properties come in a wide range of types, each with its unique characteristics, advantages, and challenges. Understanding the different types of commercial properties is essential for investors, developers, and property owners to make informed decisions about buying, selling, and managing commercial properties.

Chapter 3:

Benefits and Risks of Investing in Commercial Real Estate

Commercial real estate investing can offer a range of benefits, from generating rental income and long-term appreciation in property value to providing tax benefits and diversification. However, it also comes with its own set of risks, including market fluctuations, tenant vacancies, and regulatory changes. In this chapter, we'll explore the benefits and risks of investing in commercial real estate.

3.1 **Benefits of Investing in Commercial Real Estate**

Investing in commercial real estate can offer a range of benefits, including:

1. Rental Income: Commercial properties can generate rental income through leases with tenants.

2. Long-term Appreciation: Commercial properties can appreciate in value over time, providing a potential long-term return on investment.

3. Tax Benefits: Commercial real estate investing can provide tax benefits, such as depreciation and interest deductions.

4. Diversification: Adding commercial real estate to a diversified investment portfolio can help reduce risk and increase potential returns.

5. Physical Asset: Commercial real estate is a physical asset that can provide a sense of security and control.

3.2 **Risks of Investing in Commercial Real Estate**

While commercial real estate investing can offer many benefits, it also comes with its own set of risks, including:

1. Market Fluctuations: Commercial real estate markets can be subject to fluctuations in supply and demand, which can impact property values and rental income.

2. Tenant Vacancies: Tenant vacancies can impact rental income and property values.

3. Regulatory Changes: Changes in laws and regulations can impact commercial real estate investing, such as changes to tax laws or zoning regulations.

4. Environmental Concerns: Commercial properties can be subject to environmental concerns, such as contamination or natural disasters.

5. Illiquidity: Commercial real estate is often an illiquid asset, meaning it can take time to sell a property and access funds.

3.3 **Mitigating Risks in Commercial Real Estate Investing**

While risks are inherent in commercial real estate investing, there are steps investors can take to mitigate these risks:

1. Conduct Thorough Research: Conducting thorough research on a property and its market can help investors make informed decisions.

2. Diversify Your Portfolio: Diversifying a commercial real estate portfolio can help reduce risk and increase potential returns.

3. Work with Experienced Professionals: Working with experienced professionals, such as commercial real estate brokers and property managers, can help investors navigate the market and mitigate risks.

4. Develop a Long-term Strategy: Developing a long-term strategy for commercial real estate investing can help investors ride out market fluctuations and achieve their investment goals.

By understanding the benefits and risks of commercial real estate investing, investors can make informed decisions and develop strategies to achieve their investment goals. It is always best to consult with a professional like an attorney or accountant.

Part 2: **Investing in Commercial Real Estate**

Investing in commercial real estate can be a savvy and rewarding strategy for investors seeking to diversify their portfolios and generate significant returns. Commercial properties, such as office buildings, retail centers, industrial parks, and apartment complexes, offer a tangible asset that can appreciate in value over time, while also providing a steady stream of rental income.

Benefits of Investing in Commercial Real Estate:

1. Attractive Yields: Commercial real estate investments can generate attractive yields, often ranging from 5-30% per annum, depending on the property type, location, and market conditions.
2. Tax Benefits: Commercial real estate investments can provide tax benefits, such as depreciation, interest deductions, and potential opportunity- zone tax-deferred exchanges.
3. Diversification: Adding commercial real estate to a diversified investment portfolio can help reduce risk and increase potential returns.
4. Physical Asset: Commercial real estate is a tangible asset that can provide a sense of security and control.
5. Potential for Long-term Appreciation: Commercial properties can appreciate in value over time, providing a potential long-term return on investment.

Types of Commercial Real Estate Investments:

1. Direct Property Investment: Investing directly in a commercial property, either individually or through a partnership.

2. Real Estate Investment Trusts (REITs): Investing in a REIT, which allows individuals to invest in a diversified portfolio of commercial properties.
3. Real Estate Crowdfunding: Investing in commercial real estate through crowdfunding platforms, which allow individuals to invest in specific projects or properties.
4. Real Estate Mutual Funds: Investing in a mutual fund that focuses on commercial real estate investments.

Key Considerations for Commercial Real Estate Investing:

1. Market Research: Conducting thorough market research to understand the local market conditions, demand, and supply.
2. Property Selection: Carefully selecting a property that meets investment objectives, such as location, property type, and condition.
3. Due Diligence: Conducting thorough due diligence to understand the property's financials, legal status, and potential risks.
4. Risk Management: Developing a risk management strategy to mitigate potential

risks, such as market fluctuations, tenant vacancies, and regulatory changes.

5. Property Management: Ensuring effective property management to maintain the property's value and generate rental income.

By understanding and consulting with an attorney or an advisor the benefits, types, and key considerations of commercial real estate investing, investors can make informed decisions and capitalize on the potential rewards of this asset class.

Chapter 4:

Understanding Commercial Real Estate Markets and Working with Government

Commercial real estate markets are complex and dynamic, influenced by a wide range of factors, including economic trends, demographic changes, and government policies. To navigate these markets successfully, it's essential to understand the key characteristics and trends shaping commercial real estate, as well as the role of government in regulating and influencing these markets.

4.1 **Market Cycles**

Commercial real estate markets, like other investment markets, are subject to cycles of growth, stagnation, and decline.
Understanding these cycles can help investors anticipate potential risks and opportunities.

- Expansion Phase: Characterized by increasing demand, rising rents, and growing property values.
- Peak Phase: Marked by high property values, low vacancy rates, and intense competition for assets.
- Contraction Phase: Characterized by decreasing demand, falling rents, and declining property values.
- Trough Phase: Marked by low property values, high vacancy rates, and reduced investment activity.

4.2 **Market Fundamentals**

Understanding the fundamental drivers of commercial real estate markets is crucial for making informed investment decisions. Key market fundamentals include:

- Supply and Demand: The balance between the availability of commercial space and the demand for it.
- Economic Growth: The overall health of the economy, including factors such as GDP growth, employment rates, and consumer spending.
- Demographic Trends: Changes in population demographics, such as aging, urbanization, and migration patterns.
- Government Policies: Regulations, tax laws, and other government policies that impact commercial real estate markets.

4.3 **Working with Government**

Government plays a significant role in shaping commercial real estate markets through regulations, tax policies, and economic development initiatives. Understanding how to work effectively with government can help investors navigate these markets successfully.

- Zoning and Land-Use Regulations: Understanding local zoning and land-use regulations can help investors identify potential development opportunities and avoid costly mistakes.
- Tax Incentives: Government tax incentives, such as tax abatements and credits, can help investors reduce their tax liability and increase their returns.
- Economic Development Initiatives: Government economic development initiatives, such as business parks and enterprise zones, can provide investors with access to funding, tax incentives, and other resources.
- Public-Private Partnerships: Collaborating with government through public-private partnerships can provide investors with access to funding, expertise, and other resources.

4.4 **Navigating Government Regulations**

Navigating government regulations can be complex and time-consuming. Here are some tips for investors:

- Understand Local Regulations: Familiarize yourself with local zoning and land-use regulations, as well as other relevant laws and regulations.

- Build Relationships: Build relationships with local government officials, including planners, zoning administrators, and economic development officials.
- Seek Professional Advice: Seek professional advice from attorneys, accountants, and other experts who are familiar with local regulations and laws.
- Stay Up-to-Date: Stay up-to-date with changes in government regulations and policies that may impact your investments.

By understanding commercial real estate markets and working effectively with government, investors can navigate these complex markets successfully and achieve their investment goals.

Chapter 9:

Site Selection, Acquisition, and Future Plan Development

Site selection, acquisition, and future plan development are critical components of any commercial real estate project. The right site, acquired at the right price, and developed with a clear plan, can make all the difference in the success of a project.

9.1 Site Selection Criteria

When evaluating potential sites for a commercial real estate project, there are several key criteria to consider:

- Location: The site's proximity to transportation hubs, amenities, and target markets.
- Zoning and Land-Use Regulations: The site's zoning and land-use designation, and any potential restrictions or limitations.
- Environmental Factors: The site's environmental conditions, including any potential hazards or liabilities.

- Accessibility and Visibility: The site's accessibility and visibility, including its proximity to major roads and highways.
- Utilities and Infrastructure: The site's access to essential utilities and infrastructure, including water, sewer, electricity, and telecommunications.

9.2 **Site Acquisition Strategies**

Once a potential site has been identified, there are several strategies that can be employed to acquire the site:

- Direct Purchase: Purchasing the site directly from the owner.
- Option Agreement: Entering into an option agreement with the owner, which grants the buyer the right to purchase the site at a later date.
- Lease Option: Entering into a lease option agreement with the owner, which grants the buyer the right to lease the site with an option to purchase.
- Joint Venture: Partnering with the owner or other investors to acquire and develop the site.

9.3 Due Diligence

Before acquiring a site, it is essential to conduct thorough due diligence to identify any potential risks or liabilities:

- Title Search: Conducting a title search to verify the owner's title to the property.
- Environmental Assessment: Conducting an environmental assessment to identify any potential environmental hazards or liabilities.
- Zoning and Land-Use Analysis: Analyzing the site's zoning and land-use designation to ensure that it is compatible with the proposed project.
- Inspections and Testing: Conducting inspections and testing to identify any potential physical or structural issues with the site.

9.4 Future Plan Development

Once the site has been acquired, the next step is to develop a comprehensive plan for the site's future development:

- Market Analysis: Conducting a market analysis to identify the site's highest and best use.
- Site Planning: Developing a site plan that takes into account the site's topography, zoning and land-use regulations, and environmental factors.
- Entitlements: Obtaining any necessary entitlements, including zoning approvals, building permits, and environmental permits.
- Design and Engineering: Developing a design and engineering plan for the site, including any necessary infrastructure improvements.

By carefully evaluating potential sites, employing effective acquisition strategies, conducting thorough due diligence, and developing a comprehensive plan for future development, investors and developers can minimize risks and maximize returns on their commercial real estate investments.

Chapter 10:

Entitlements and Approvals

Entitlements and approvals are a critical component of any commercial real estate development project. Obtaining the necessary entitlements and approvals can be a complex and time-consuming process, requiring careful planning, coordination, and communication with various stakeholders.

10.1 **Types of Entitlements**

There are several types of entitlements that may be required for a commercial real estate development project, including:

- Zoning Approvals: Approval from local government to develop a property in accordance with local zoning regulations.
- Building Permits: Approval from local government to construct a building or other structure.
- Environmental Permits: Approval from local, state, or federal government to develop a property that may impact the environment.

- Special Use Permits: Approval from local government to develop a property for a specific use, such as a restaurant or nightclub.

10.2 **Entitlement Process**

The entitlement process typically involves several steps, including:

- Pre-Application Meetings: Meetings with local government officials to discuss the proposed project and identify potential issues.
- Application Submission: Submission of a formal application for entitlements, including all required plans, specifications, and other documentation.
- Review and Comment: Review of the application by local government officials, with comments and feedback provided to the applicant.
- Public Hearings: Public hearings to consider the proposed project and receive input from the community.
- Approval or Denial: Final approval or denial of the entitlement application.

10.3 **Strategies for Obtaining Entitlements**

Obtaining entitlements can be a challenging and time-consuming process. Here are some strategies for success:

- Early Engagement: Engaging with local government officials and other stakeholders early in the process to build relationships and identify potential issues.
- Community Outreach: Conducting community outreach and education to build support for the proposed project.
- Collaboration with Neighboring Property Owners: Collaborating with neighboring property owners to address concerns and build support for the proposed project.
- Flexibility and Adaptability: Being flexible and adaptable throughout the entitlement process, and willing to make changes to the proposed project as needed.

10.4 **Common Challenges and Solutions**

Obtaining entitlements can be a complex and challenging process. Here are some common challenges and solutions:

- Neighborhood Opposition: Addressing concerns and building support through community outreach and education.
- Environmental Concerns: Conducting environmental studies and developing strategies to mitigate potential impacts.
- Zoning and Land-Use Issues: Working with local government officials to identify potential zoning and land-use issues, and developing strategies to address them.

By understanding the entitlement process, employing effective strategies for obtaining entitlements, and being prepared to address common challenges, developers and investors can minimize risks and maximize returns on their commercial real estate investments.

Chapter 11:

Construction, Project Management, Demolition, and Insurance

Construction is a critical phase of any commercial real estate development project. Effective project management, demolition (if required), and insurance are essential components of a successful construction project.

11.1 Construction Process

The construction process typically involves the following steps:

- Pre-Construction: Finalizing plans and specifications, obtaining necessary permits, and hiring contractors and subcontractors.
- Site Preparation: Clearing the land, excavating the site, and preparing the foundation.
- Building Construction: Constructing the building, including installing electrical, plumbing, and HVAC systems.

- Finishing Work: Installing finishes, such as flooring, walls, and ceilings.
- Final Inspections and Occupancy: Conducting final inspections and obtaining a certificate of occupancy.

11.2 **Project Management**

Effective project management is critical to ensuring that the construction process is completed on time, within budget, and to the required quality standards. Key aspects of project management include:

- Project Planning: Defining project scope, goals, and timelines.
- Budgeting and Cost Management: Establishing a budget and managing costs throughout the project.
- Scheduling: Creating a project schedule and managing timelines.
- Risk Management: Identifying and mitigating potential risks.
- Quality Control: Ensuring that the project meets the required quality standards.

11.3 **Demolition**

Demolition may be required if an existing structure needs to be removed to make way for the new development. Key considerations for demolition include:

- Environmental Hazards: Identifying and mitigating potential environmental hazards, such as asbestos or lead paint.
- Structural Integrity: Ensuring that the structure is safe to demolish and that adjacent properties are not damaged.
- Permitting and Approvals: Obtaining necessary permits and approvals before commencing demolition.

11.4 **Insurance**

Insurance is an essential component of any construction project. Key types of insurance include:

- Liability Insurance: Protecting against claims for damages or injuries.
- Property Insurance: Protecting against damage to the property.

- Workers' Compensation Insurance: Providing coverage for workers injured on the job.
- Performance Bonds: Guaranteeing that the contractor will complete the project.

11.5 **Construction Risks and Mitigation Strategies**

Construction projects are inherently risky, with potential risks including:

- Delays and Cost Overruns: Mitigated through effective project management and contingency planning.
- Design and Construction Defects: Mitigated through quality control and assurance processes.
- Environmental Hazards: Mitigated through environmental assessments and remediation.
- Labor Disputes and Strikes: Mitigated through effective labor relations and contingency planning.

By understanding the construction process, project management, demolition, and insurance, developers and investors can minimize risks and maximize returns on their commercial real estate investments.

Chapter 12:

Redevelopment, Repositioning, and Replacing of Commercial Properties

Redevelopment, repositioning, and replacing of commercial properties are strategies used to revitalize and reinvigorate existing properties, increasing their value and potential for returns. This chapter will explore these strategies in depth.

12.1 **Redevelopment**

Redevelopment involves renovating or reconfiguring an existing property to increase its value and appeal. This can include:

- Cosmetic Upgrades: Updating the property's exterior and interior appearance.
- Mechanical Upgrades: Upgrading the property's mechanical systems, such as HVAC and plumbing.
- Structural Repairs: Repairing or replacing the property's structural elements.

12.2 **Repositioning**

Repositioning involves rebranding or reimagining an existing property to appeal to a new target market or demographic. This can include:

- Rebranding: Changing the property's name, logo, and marketing materials.
- Redesigning: Redesigning the property's layout, amenities, and services.
- Repricing: Adjusting the property's pricing strategy to appeal to the new target market.

12.3 **Replacing**

Replacing involves demolishing an existing property and building a new one in its place. This can include:

- Demolition: Demolishing the existing property.
- Site Preparation: Preparing the site for new construction.
- New Construction: Building a new property on the site.

12.4 **Benefits and Challenges**

Redevelopment, repositioning, and replacing can offer numerous benefits, including:

- Increased Value: Increasing the property's value and potential for returns.
- Improved Appeal: Enhancing the property's appeal to tenants, customers, or investors.
- Competitive Advantage: Gaining a competitive advantage in the market.

However, these strategies also present challenges, including:

- Cost and Budgeting: Managing costs and budgets for redevelopment, repositioning, or replacing.
- Regulatory Approvals: Obtaining necessary regulatory approvals and permits.
- Tenant or Customer Disruption: Minimizing disruption to tenants or customers during redevelopment or repositioning.

12.5 **Case Studies**

Here are some case studies illustrating successful redevelopment, repositioning, and replacing of commercial properties:

- Redevelopment of a Shopping Mall: Redeveloping a struggling shopping mall into a thriving mixed-use development.
- Repositioning of an Office Building: Repositioning an outdated office building into a modern, amenity-rich workspace.
- Replacing a Historic Building: Replacing a historic building with a new, sustainable development that incorporates historic elements.

By understanding the strategies and benefits of redevelopment, repositioning, and replacing, commercial property owners and investors can unlock new value and potential for returns in their existing properties.

Part 4: **Property Management and Operations**

Effective property management and operations are the backbone of any successful commercial real estate investment. They play a critical role in maximizing the value and potential of a property, while also ensuring the satisfaction and retention of tenants. This part will provide a comprehensive overview of the key concepts, strategies, and best practices for managing and operating commercial properties.

By mastering the concepts and strategies outlined in this part, commercial real estate investors and property managers can optimize property performance, enhance tenant satisfaction, and maximize returns on investment. Effective property management and operations are essential to achieving success in the commercial real estate industry.

Chapter 13:

Introduction to Commercial Property Management

13.1 **Overview of Commercial Property Management**

Commercial property management is the process of overseeing and managing commercial properties, including office buildings, retail centers, industrial parks, and apartment complexes. Effective commercial property management involves a range of activities, including:

- Managing the day-to-day operations of the property
- Maintaining the physical condition of the property
- Managing tenant relationships and lease agreements
- Collecting rent and managing finances
- Ensuring compliance with laws and regulations

13.2 Key Players in Commercial Property Management

Several key players are involved in commercial property management, including:

- Property owners: Individuals or companies that own the commercial property.
- Property managers: Individuals or companies responsible for overseeing the day-to-day operations of the property.
- Tenants: Businesses or individuals that lease space in the commercial property.
- Leasing agents: Individuals or companies responsible for marketing and leasing available space in the property.

13.3 Benefits of Effective Commercial Property Management

Effective commercial property management offers numerous benefits, including:

- Increased property value: Well-managed properties tend to increase in value over time.
- Improved cash flow: Effective property management can help to maximize rental income and minimize expenses.

- Enhanced tenant satisfaction: Happy tenants are more likely to renew their leases and recommend the property to others.
- Reduced risk: Effective property management can help to minimize the risk of property damage, liability, and other potential issues.

13.4 Challenges Facing Commercial Property Managers

Commercial property managers face a range of challenges, including:

- Managing complex tenant relationships
- Staying up-to-date with changing laws and regulations
- Maintaining the physical condition of the property
- Managing finances and ensuring profitability
- Adapting to changing market conditions and trends.

13.5 Best Practices in Commercial Property Management

To be successful, commercial property managers should follow best practices, including:

- Developing a comprehensive property management plan
- Establishing clear communication channels with tenants and stakeholders
- Conducting regular property inspections and maintenance
- Staying up-to-date with industry trends and best practices
- Fostering a positive and respectful work environment.

Chapter 14:

Leasing and Tenant Relations

14.1 Overview of Leasing and Tenant Relations

Leasing and tenant relations are critical components of commercial property management. A well-structured lease agreement and positive tenant relationships can help to ensure the long-term success and profitability of a commercial property.

14.2 Types of Leases

There are several types of leases used in commercial property management, including:

- Gross Lease: A lease in which the landlord pays all expenses, including property taxes, insurance, and maintenance.
- Net Lease: A lease in which the tenant pays a portion of the expenses, such as property taxes and insurance.

- Triple Net Lease: A lease in which the tenant pays all expenses, including property taxes, insurance, and maintenance.
- Percentage Lease: A lease in which the tenant pays a percentage of their gross sales as rent.

14.3 **Key Components of a Lease Agreement**

A well-structured lease agreement should include the following key components:

- Rent and payment terms
- Lease duration and renewal options
- Security deposit and damage provisions
- Maintenance and repair responsibilities
- Insurance and liability provisions
- Dispute resolution and termination clauses

14.4 **Tenant Relations and Communication**

Positive tenant relations and effective communication are essential for maintaining a successful commercial property. This includes:

- Responding promptly to tenant inquiries and concerns
- Providing regular updates on property maintenance and repairs
- Offering amenities and services that enhance the tenant experience
- Fostering a positive and respectful landlord-tenant relationship

14.5 **Lease Administration and Renewal Strategies**

Effective lease administration and renewal strategies are critical for maintaining a stable and profitable commercial property. This includes:

- Tracking lease expiration dates and renewal options
- Negotiating lease renewals and rent increases
- Managing lease amendments and terminations
- Maintaining accurate and up-to-date lease records

14.6 **Tenant Retention Strategies**

Tenant retention is critical for maintaining a successful commercial property. This includes:

- Providing excellent customer service and support
- Offering competitive rent rates and lease terms
- Maintaining a well-maintained and attractive property
- Fostering a positive and respectful landlord-tenant relationship

14.7 **Conflict Resolution and Dispute Management**

Conflict resolution and dispute management are essential for maintaining positive tenant relations and minimizing potential liabilities. This includes:

- Establishing clear communication channels and protocols
- Responding promptly to tenant complaints and concerns
- Negotiating disputes and resolving conflicts in a fair and timely manner
- Documenting all disputes and resolutions.

Chapter 15:

Property Maintenance and Repairs

15.1 Overview of Property Maintenance and Repairs

Property maintenance and repairs are essential components of commercial property management. A well-maintained property can help to:

- Preserve property value
- Attract and retain tenants
- Minimize repair costs
- Ensure compliance with laws and regulations

15.2 Types of Property Maintenance

There are several types of property maintenance, including:

- Routine maintenance: Regular tasks such as cleaning, trash removal, and landscaping.
- Preventative maintenance: Scheduled tasks such as HVAC maintenance, plumbing inspections, and roof repairs.

- Corrective maintenance: Repairs made in response to a specific problem or issue.
- Predictive maintenance: Using data and analytics to predict and prevent potential maintenance issues.

15.3 **Property Inspection and Assessment**

Regular property inspections and assessments are crucial for identifying potential maintenance issues and prioritizing repairs. This includes:

- Visual inspections of the property and its systems
- Review of maintenance records and repair history
- Identification of potential safety hazards and liabilities
- Development of a prioritized maintenance and repair plan

15.4 **Maintenance and Repair Strategies**

Effective maintenance and repair strategies are essential for minimizing costs and ensuring the long-term viability of the property. This includes:

- Developing a comprehensive maintenance and repair plan
- Establishing a preventative maintenance schedule
- Identifying and addressing potential safety hazards and liabilities
- Coordinating repairs and maintenance with tenants and stakeholders

15.5 **Budgeting for Maintenance and Repairs**

Budgeting for maintenance and repairs is critical for ensuring the financial viability of the property. This includes:

- Developing a comprehensive maintenance and repair budget
- Identifying and prioritizing maintenance and repair needs
- Establishing a reserve fund for unexpected repairs and expenses
- Reviewing and updating the budget regularly

15.6 Hiring and Managing Maintenance and Repair Contractors

Hiring and managing maintenance and repair contractors is essential for ensuring that work is completed efficiently and effectively. This includes:

- Developing a comprehensive contractor selection and management plan
- Establishing clear communication channels and protocols
- Defining scope of work and expectations
- Monitoring and evaluating contractor performance

15.7 Sustainability and Energy Efficiency

Sustainability and energy efficiency are increasingly important considerations in commercial property management. This includes:

- Implementing energy-efficient technologies and strategies
- Reducing water consumption and implementing water-efficient technologies

- Implementing recycling and waste reduction programs
- Promoting sustainable practices and behaviors among tenants and stakeholders.

Chapter 16:

Financial Management and Accounting for Commercial Properties

16.1 Overview of Financial Management and Accounting

Effective financial management and accounting are critical components of commercial property management. Accurate financial reporting and analysis enable property owners and managers to make informed decisions, optimize property performance, and maximize returns on investment.

16.2 Financial Statements for Commercial Properties

There are several key financial statements used in commercial property management, including:

- Balance Sheet: A snapshot of the property's financial position at a given point in time.

- Income Statement: A summary of the property's revenues and expenses over a specific period.
- Cash Flow Statement: A summary of the property's inflows and outflows of cash over a specific period.

16.3 Accounting Principles and Standards

Commercial property accounting is guided by several key principles and standards, including:

- Generally Accepted Accounting Principles (GAAP)
- Financial Accounting Standards Board (FASB)
- International Financial Reporting Standards (IFRS)

16.4 Budgeting and Forecasting

Budgeting and forecasting are essential components of commercial property financial management. This includes:

- Developing a comprehensive budget and forecasting plan

- Identifying and prioritizing revenue and expense items
- Establishing a system for tracking and analyzing budget variances
- Reviewing and updating the budget regularly

16.5 Cash Management and Funding

Effective cash management and funding are critical for ensuring the financial viability of a commercial property. This includes:

- Managing cash inflows and outflows
- Maintaining a cash reserve fund
- Identifying and securing funding sources
- Negotiating loan terms and conditions

16.6 Taxation and Depreciation

Taxation and depreciation are important considerations in commercial property financial management. This includes:

- Understanding tax laws and regulations
- Calculating depreciation and amortization
- Maximizing tax benefits and deductions
- Minimizing tax liabilities and penalties

16.7 Financial Analysis and Performance Metrics

Financial analysis and performance metrics are essential for evaluating the financial performance of a commercial property. This includes:

- Calculating key performance metrics such as net operating income (NOI) and capitalization rate
- Analyzing financial statements and trends
- Identifying areas for improvement and optimization
- Developing strategies for enhancing financial performance.

Part 5: **Advanced Topics and Trends**

This part will explore advanced topics and trends in commercial real estate, including sustainable development, technology and innovation, fractional investing and global market trends.

Chapter 17:

Sustainable and Energy-Efficient Commercial Properties

17.1 Overview of Sustainable and Energy-Efficient Commercial Properties

Sustainable and energy-efficient commercial properties are designed to minimize their impact on the environment while also reducing operating costs and improving occupant health and productivity. This chapter will explore the principles and practices of sustainable and energy-efficient commercial property development and management.

17.2 Benefits of Sustainable and Energy-Efficient Commercial Properties

Sustainable and energy-efficient commercial properties offer numerous benefits, including:

- Reduced energy consumption and greenhouse gas emissions
- Lower operating costs and increased profitability

- Improved occupant health and productivity
- Enhanced brand reputation and marketability
- Compliance with environmental regulations and standards

17.3 Sustainable Design and Development Principles

Sustainable design and development principles are critical to creating energy-efficient and environmentally friendly commercial properties. These principles include:

- Integrating natural light and ventilation
- Using sustainable and recycled materials
- Implementing energy-efficient systems and technologies
- Incorporating green spaces and landscaping
- Designing for adaptability and flexibility

17.4 Energy-Efficient Systems and Technologies

Energy-efficient systems and technologies are essential to reducing energy consumption and greenhouse gas emissions in commercial properties. These systems and technologies include:

- LED lighting and smart lighting controls
- High-efficiency HVAC systems and controls
- Energy-recovery systems and heat pumps
- Solar panels and renewable energy systems
- Energy management systems and monitoring tools

17.5 Green Building Certifications and Standards

Green building certifications and standards provide a framework for evaluating and recognizing sustainable and energy-efficient commercial properties. These certifications and standards include:

- LEED (Leadership in Energy and Environmental Design)
- Energy Star
- Green Globes
- WELL Building Standard
- Passive House Standard

17.6 Best Practices for Sustainable and Energy-Efficient Property Management

Best practices for sustainable and energy-efficient property management include:

- Conducting regular energy audits and assessments
- Implementing energy-efficient practices and procedures
- Engaging with occupants and stakeholders on sustainability initiatives
- Monitoring and reporting on sustainability performance
- Continuously evaluating and improving sustainability strategies and practices.

Chapter 18:

Technology and Innovation in Commercial Real Estate

18.1 Overview of Technology and Innovation in Commercial Real Estate

Technology and innovation are transforming the commercial real estate industry, enabling owners, investors, and occupiers to optimize their properties, streamline operations, and enhance decision-making. This chapter will explore the latest technologies and innovations shaping the commercial real estate landscape.

18.2 Prop-Tech: The Intersection of Property and Technology

Prop-Tech, short for property technology, refers to the application of technology to the property industry. Prop-Tech encompasses a wide range of innovations, including:

- Property management software
- Online marketplaces and listing platforms
- Virtual and augmented reality

- Artificial intelligence and machine learning
- Block-chain and distributed ledger technology

18.3 Smart Buildings and Intelligent Infrastructure

Smart buildings and intelligent infrastructure are revolutionizing the way commercial properties are designed, constructed, and operated. Key features of smart buildings include:

- Energy-efficient systems and controls
- Advanced lighting and HVAC systems
- Intelligent security and access control systems
- High-speed data and communication networks
- Integrated building management systems

18.4 Data Analytics and Business Intelligence

Data analytics and business intelligence are essential for commercial real estate professionals to make informed decisions, optimize property performance, and drive business growth. Key applications of data analytics include:

- Market analysis and trend forecasting
- Property valuation and appraisal
- Tenant and occupier analysis
- Energy and resource consumption analysis
- Risk management and mitigation

18.5 Emerging Trends and Innovations

The commercial real estate industry is constantly evolving, with new trends and innovations emerging regularly. Some of the most exciting developments include:

- Artificial intelligence and machine learning
- Block-chain and distributed ledger technology
- Virtual and augmented reality
- Internet of Things (IoT) and smart buildings
- Electric and autonomous vehicles

18.6 Best Practices for Implementing Technology and Innovation

To successfully implement technology and innovation in commercial real estate, professionals should follow best practices, including:

- Conducting thorough needs assessments and gap analyses
- Developing clear business cases and ROI analyses
- Selecting the right technology and innovation partners
- Providing comprehensive training and support
- Continuously monitoring and evaluating technology and innovation performance.

Chapter 19:

Impact of Economic and Market Trends on Commercial Real Estate

19.1 Overview of Economic and Market Trends

Economic and market trends have a significant impact on the commercial real estate industry. Understanding these trends is crucial for investors, developers, and property managers to make informed decisions and navigate the market. This chapter will explore the key economic and market trends affecting commercial real estate.

19.2 Economic Trends Affecting Commercial Real Estate

Several economic trends have a significant impact on commercial real estate, including:

- GDP and Economic Growth: A strong economy with high GDP growth tends to drive demand for commercial space.

- Interest Rates: Changes in interest rates can impact borrowing costs, property values, and investment decisions.
- Inflation: Rising inflation can lead to increased construction costs, property values, and rental rates.
- Unemployment: Low unemployment rates can drive demand for commercial space, particularly in the office and retail sectors.

19.3 Market Trends Affecting Commercial Real Estate

Several market trends are also impacting commercial real estate, including:

- Shift to Omni-channel Retail: The rise of e-commerce has led to a shift towards omni-channel retail, with retailers seeking flexible and adaptable spaces.
- Growing Demand for Co-working and Flexible Office Space: The gig economy and changing workforce demographics have driven demand for co-working and flexible office space.
- Increasing Focus on Sustainability and Energy Efficiency: Investors, tenants, and property managers are increasingly prioritizing

sustainability and energy efficiency in commercial real estate.
- Advancements in Technology and Automation: Technological advancements are transforming the commercial real estate industry, from property management and leasing to construction and design.

19.4 Impact of Demographic Trends on Commercial Real Estate

Demographic trends are also having a significant impact on commercial real estate, including:

- Aging Population: The aging population is driving demand for healthcare and senior housing facilities.
- Urbanization: The trend towards urbanization is driving demand for mixed-use developments, multifamily housing, and urban office space.
- Changing Workforce Demographics: The changing workforce demographics are driving demand for flexible and adaptable office space.

19.5 Best Practices for Navigating Economic and Market Trends

To successfully navigate economic and market trends, commercial real estate professionals should follow best practices, including:

- Staying informed about market trends and economic conditions
- Conducting thorough market research and analysis
- Developing flexible and adaptable business strategies
- Building strong relationships with tenants, investors, and partners
- Continuously monitoring and evaluating market trends and economic conditions.

Chapter 20:

Future of Commercial Real Estate: Trends and Opportunities

20.1 Overview of the Future of Commercial Real Estate

The commercial real estate industry is undergoing significant transformations, driven by technological advancements, shifting demographics, Real time market making for real estate property and changing workforce needs. This chapter will explore the trends and opportunities shaping the future of commercial real estate.

20.2 **Emerging Trends in Commercial Real Estate**

Several emerging trends are expected to shape the future of commercial real estate, including:

- Increased focus on sustainability and energy efficiency
- Growing demand for flexible and adaptable office space

- Integration of technology and automation in property management and operations
- Shift towards experiential and amenity-rich retail spaces
- Growing importance of data analytics and business intelligence in decision-making

20.3 Impact of Technology on Commercial Real Estate

Technology is transforming the commercial real estate industry, enabling greater efficiency, transparency, and innovation. Key technological trends include:

- Artificial intelligence and machine learning
- Internet of Things (IoT) and smart buildings
- Block-chain and distributed ledger technology
- Virtual and augmented reality
- 5G networks and edge computing

20.4 Changing Workforce Demographics and Needs

The changing workforce demographics and needs are driving demand for new types of commercial spaces, including:

- Flexible and adaptable office spaces
- Co-working and shared office spaces
- Wellness-focused and amenity-rich office spaces
- Urban and mixed-use developments

20.5 Opportunities for Innovation and Growth

The future of commercial real estate presents numerous opportunities for innovation and growth, including:

- Developing sustainable and energy-efficient buildings
- Creating flexible and adaptable office spaces
- Integrating technology and automation in property management and operations
- Developing experiential and amenity-rich retail spaces
- Providing data-driven insights and analytics to inform decision-making

20.6 Best Practices for Preparing for the Future of Commercial Real Estate

To prepare for the future of commercial real estate, professionals should follow best practices, including:

- Staying informed about emerging trends and technologies
- Developing flexible and adaptable business strategies
- Investing in data analytics and business intelligence
- Focusing on sustainability and energy efficiency
- Building strong relationships with tenants, investors, and partners.

Putting a REIT on the block-chain can provide numerous benefits, including:

Increased Efficiency

1. Automated processes: Smart contracts can automate various processes, such as dividend distributions, voting, and compliance.
2. Reduced paperwork: Block-chain-based REITs can reduce paperwork and administrative burdens associated with traditional REITs.

Improved Transparency

1. Real-time updates: Block-chain technology provides real-time updates on REIT performance, allowing investors to make informed decisions.
2. Transparent ownership: Block-chain-based REITs provide transparent ownership records, reducing the risk of fraud and errors.

Enhanced Security

1. Immutable records: Block-chain technology provides immutable records, ensuring that REIT data is tamper-proof and secure.
2. Secure transactions: Smart contracts can facilitate secure transactions, reducing the risk of fraud and errors.

Increased Liquidity

1. Tokenization: Block-chain-based REITs can tokenize their assets, providing increased liquidity and flexibility for investors.
2. Secondary markets: Block-chain-based REITs can create secondary markets for their tokens,

providing investors with a way to buy and sell tokens.

Reduced Costs

1. Lower administrative costs: Block-chain-based REITs can reduce administrative costs associated with traditional REITs.
2. Lower transaction costs: Smart contracts can facilitate secure and efficient transactions, reducing transaction costs.

Improved Compliance

1. Automated compliance: Smart contracts can automate compliance with regulatory requirements, reducing the risk of non-compliance.
2. Transparent reporting: Block-chain-based REITs can provide transparent reporting, ensuring compliance with regulatory requirements.

Increased Investor Access

1. Global access: Block-chain-based REITs can provide global access to investors, increasing the potential investor base.

2. Lower investment minimums: Block-chain-based REITs can provide lower investment minimums, increasing access to investors who may not have been able to invest in traditional REITs.

Opportunity Zone (OZ) REITs offer several benefits to investors, including:

Tax Benefits

1. Temporary deferral of capital gains: Investors can defer capital gains taxes on proceeds invested in an OZ REIT.
2. Partial reduction of capital gains: If investors hold their OZ REIT investment for at least 5 years, they can reduce their capital gains tax liability by 10%.
3. Zero capital gains tax: If investors hold their OZ REIT investment for at least 10 years, they can eliminate their capital gains tax liability.

Economic Benefits

1. Job creation and economic growth: OZ REITs invest in economically distressed areas, promoting job creation and economic growth.

2. Community development: OZ REITs can invest in community development projects, such as affordable housing, schools, and healthcare facilities.

Investment Benefits

1. Diversification: OZ REITs offer a unique investment opportunity, allowing investors to diversify their portfolios.
2. Potential for long-term appreciation: OZ REITs invest in areas with potential for long-term economic growth, which can lead to appreciation in property values.
3. Rental income: OZ REITs can generate rental income, providing a potential source of regular returns.

Regulatory Benefits

1. Flexibility: OZ REITs have flexibility in their investment strategies, allowing them to adapt to changing market conditions.
2. Streamlined regulatory process: The OZ program provides a streamlined regulatory process, reducing the administrative burden on OZ REITs.

Examples of Opportunity Zone REITs:

1. Fund-rise Opportunity Zone REIT: A REIT that invests in OZ properties, offering a diversified portfolio and potential for long-term appreciation.
2. Rich Uncles Opportunity Zone REIT: A REIT that invests in OZ properties, offering a potential source of regular returns through rental income.
3. Cresset Partners Opportunity Zone REIT: A REIT that invests in OZ properties, offering a diversified portfolio and potential for long-term appreciation.
4. Blue Water Holding Group real estate investment trust Opportunity zone REIT offers a diversified portfolio with many verticals and potential for long-term appreciation and returns.

Distributive concepts and building methods are innovative approaches to construction that focus on decentralized, modular, and prefabricated building techniques. Here are some key concepts and methods:

Distributive Concepts

1. Modular Construction: Buildings are constructed in a factory, transported to the site, and assembled.
2. Prefabricated Construction: Building components, such as walls, roofs, and floors, are prefabricated in a factory and assembled on-site.
3. Panelized Construction: Building panels, including walls, floors, and roofs, are prefabricated and assembled on-site.
4. Kit-of-Parts Construction: A kit of prefabricated building components is assembled on-site to form a building.

Building Methods

1. 3D Printing: Buildings are constructed using 3D printing technology, which deposits materials layer by layer.

2. Structural Insulated Panels (SIPs): Buildings are constructed using SIPs, which consist of an insulating foam core sandwiched between two structural facings.

3. Cross-Laminated Timber (CLT): Buildings are constructed using CLT, which consists of layers of wood laminated together.

4. Insulated Concrete Forms (ICFs): Buildings are constructed using ICFs, which consist of hollow blocks or panels made of insulating material.

Benefits

1. Increased Efficiency: Distributive concepts and building methods can reduce construction time and increase efficiency.

2. Improved Quality: Prefabricated and modular construction can improve quality by reducing on-site errors and variability.

3. Reduced Waste: Distributive concepts and building methods can reduce waste by using prefabricated components and minimizing on-site construction.

4. Increased Sustainability: Distributive concepts and building methods can promote sustainability by using recycled materials,

reducing energy consumption, and minimizing environmental impact.

Examples

1. Katerra: A construction company that uses modular construction and prefabricated components to build homes and commercial buildings.
2. Module: A construction company that uses modular construction to build homes and commercial buildings.
3. Win-Sun: A Chinese construction company that uses 3D printing to build homes and commercial buildings.
4. Lend-lease: A construction company that uses prefabricated construction and modular building techniques to build homes and commercial buildings.

Advanced Building Materials and Concepts

Introduction

The construction industry has witnessed significant advancements in recent years, driven by the need for sustainable, energy-efficient, and resilient buildings. This chapter explores some of the advanced building materials and concepts that are transforming the industry.

Advanced Building Materials

1. Green Concrete

Green concrete, also known as sustainable concrete, is made from environmentally friendly materials such as recycled aggregates, fly ash, and slag cement. It reduces greenhouse gas emissions, conserves natural resources, and provides improved durability.

2. Cross-Laminated Timber (CLT)

CLT is a type of engineered wood made from layers of timber boards stacked perpendicular to each other. It offers excellent strength, stability, and thermal insulation, making it an ideal material for building frames, walls, and roofs.

3. Fiber-Reinforced Polymers (FRP)

FRP is a composite material made from fibers such as carbon, glass, or basalt, embedded in a polymer matrix. It provides exceptional strength-to-weight ratio, corrosion resistance, and durability, making it suitable for building facades, roofs, and structural components.

4. Transparent Aluminum

Transparent aluminum, also known as aluminum oxy-nitride, is a transparent ceramic material that offers exceptional strength, durability, and optical clarity. It is ideal for building facades, windows, and skylights.

5. Self-Healing Concrete

Self-healing concrete is a type of concrete that can repair cracks and damages autonomously. It contains bacteria that produce calcite, a natural cement, when exposed to water and oxygen. This material can significantly reduce maintenance costs and extend the lifespan of buildings.

Advanced Building Concepts

1. Building Information Modelling (BIM)

BIM is a digital representation of a building's physical and functional characteristics. It enables architects, engineers, and contractors to collaborate and share information more effectively, reducing errors and improving construction efficiency.

2. Modular Construction

Modular construction involves assembling building components, such as walls, floors, and roofs, in a factory before transporting them to the site for assembly. This approach reduces construction time, waste, and costs, while improving quality and sustainability.

3. 3D Printing

3D printing, also known as additive manufacturing, involves creating building components or entire structures layer by layer using a digital model. This technology enables rapid construction, complex geometries, and reduced material waste.

4. Smart Buildings

Smart buildings integrate advanced technologies, such as sensors, IoT devices, and data analytics, to optimize energy efficiency, comfort, and security. They can adapt to changing environmental conditions, occupant needs, and energy prices.

5. Bio-philic Design

Bio-philic design incorporates natural elements, such as plants, daylight, and ventilation, into building design to promote occupant health, well-being, and productivity. This approach can reduce stress, improve air quality, and increase employee satisfaction.

Conclusion

The construction industry is undergoing a significant transformation, driven by advances in materials science, digital technologies, and sustainable design. The adoption of advanced building materials and concepts can help reduce environmental impacts, improve building performance, and enhance occupant experience. As the industry continues to evolve, it is essential to stay informed about the latest developments and innovations that are shaping the future of building design and construction.

Qualifying the Developer, Investor, Client, Tenant

Qualifying the developer, investor, client, or tenant is a critical step in any commercial real estate transaction. It involves evaluating their financial capacity, creditworthiness, and business reputation to determine their ability to fulfill their obligations.

Developer Qualification

When qualifying a developer, consider the following factors:

- Financial capacity: Evaluate their financial statements, credit reports, and funding sources.

- Development experience: Assess their track record of completing successful projects.
- Reputation: Research their reputation in the industry, including any past disputes or litigation.
- Business plan: Review their business plan and feasibility studies for the project.

Investor Qualification

When qualifying an investor, consider the following factors:

- Financial capacity: Evaluate their financial statements, credit reports, and investment history.
- Investment experience: Assess their track record of investing in commercial real estate.
- Risk tolerance: Determine their risk tolerance and investment goals.
- Business plan: Review their investment strategy and business plan.

Client Qualification

When qualifying a client, consider the following factors:

- Financial capacity: Evaluate their financial statements, credit reports, and funding sources.
- Business reputation: Research their reputation in the industry, including any past disputes or litigation.
- Business plan: Review their business plan and feasibility studies for the project.
- Needs and goals: Determine their needs and goals for the project.

Tenant Qualification

When qualifying a tenant, consider the following factors:

- Financial capacity: Evaluate their financial statements, credit reports, and rental history.
- Business reputation: Research their reputation in the industry, including any past disputes or litigation.

- Lease requirements: Determine their lease requirements, including term, rent, and space needs.
- Creditworthiness: Assess their creditworthiness and ability to fulfill their lease obligations.

Best Practices for Qualifying Developers, Investors, Clients, Tenants

- Verify financial information through independent sources.
- Conduct thorough background checks and research.
- Evaluate their reputation and track record in the industry.
- Assess their business plan and feasibility studies.
- Determine their needs and goals for the project.
- Establish clear communication channels and expectations.

What is a Special Purpose Vehicle (SPV) Market Maker?

A Special Purpose Vehicle (SPV) Market Maker is a type of financial entity that provides liquidity to specific assets or markets by buying and selling securities through a separate legal entity, known as a Special Purpose Vehicle (SPV).

Characteristics of an SPV Market Maker:

1. Separate Legal Entity: An SPV Market Maker operates through a separate legal entity, which is typically a subsidiary company.
2. Specific Asset Focus: An SPV Market Maker focuses on providing liquidity to specific assets, such as mortgage-backed securities, asset-backed securities, or other specialized financial instruments.
3. Market Making Activities: An SPV Market Maker engages in market making activities, including buying and selling securities, quoting prices, and providing liquidity to the market.
4. Risk Management: An SPV Market Maker employs risk management strategies to mitigate potential losses and ensure the stability of the SPV.

Benefits of an SPV Market Maker:

1. Improved Liquidity: An SPV Market Maker provides liquidity to specific assets, making it easier for investors to buy and sell securities.
2. Reduced Risk: By operating through a separate legal entity, an SPV Market Maker can isolate risks and protect the parent company's balance sheet.
3. Increased Efficiency: An SPV Market Maker can streamline market making activities, reducing costs and improving efficiency.
4. Enhanced Transparency: An SPV Market Maker provides transparent pricing and trading information, promoting market efficiency and fairness.

Examples of SPV Market Makers:

1. Mortgage-Backed Securities (MBS) Market Makers: SPV Market Makers that provide liquidity to MBS markets, enabling investors to buy and sell mortgage-backed securities.
2. Asset-Backed Securities (ABS) Market Makers: SPV Market Makers that provide liquidity to ABS markets, enabling investors to buy and sell asset-backed securities.

3. Structured Product Market Makers: SPV Market Makers that provide liquidity to structured product markets, enabling investors to buy and sell complex financial instruments.

Conclusion:

Special Purpose Vehicle (SPV) Market Makers play a vital role in providing liquidity to specific assets and markets. By operating through a separate legal entity, SPV Market Makers can isolate risks, improve efficiency, and promote market transparency. As financial markets continue to evolve, SPV Market Makers will remain essential in facilitating the buying and selling of securities.

What is a Special Purpose Vehicle (SPV) Real Estate Market Making?

A Special Purpose Vehicle (SPV) Real Estate Market Making is a type of financial entity that provides liquidity to real estate markets by buying and selling properties through a separate legal entity, known as a Special Purpose Vehicle (SPV).

Characteristics of an SPV Real Estate Market Making:

1. Separate Legal Entity: An SPV Real Estate Market Making operates through a separate legal entity, which is typically a subsidiary company.
2. Real Estate Focus: An SPV Real Estate Market Making focuses on providing liquidity to real estate markets, including residential, commercial, and industrial properties.
3. Market Making Activities: An SPV Real Estate Market Making engages in market making activities, including buying and selling properties, quoting prices, and providing liquidity to the market.
4. Risk Management: An SPV Real Estate Market Making employs risk management strategies to mitigate potential losses and ensure the stability of the SPV.

Benefits of an SPV Real Estate Market Making:

1. Improved Liquidity: An SPV Real Estate Market Making provides liquidity to real estate markets, making it easier for buyers and sellers to transact.

2. Reduced Risk: By operating through a separate legal entity, an SPV Real Estate Market Making can isolate risks and protect the parent company's balance sheet.
3. Increased Efficiency: An SPV Real Estate Market Making can streamline market making activities, reducing costs and improving efficiency.
4. Enhanced Transparency: An SPV Real Estate Market Making provides transparent pricing and trading information, promoting market efficiency and fairness.

Examples of SPV Real Estate Market Making:

1. Residential Property Market Making: SPV Real Estate Market Making that provides liquidity to residential property markets, enabling buyers and sellers to transact.
2. Commercial Property Market Making: SPV Real Estate Market Making that provides liquidity to commercial property markets, enabling businesses to buy and sell properties.
3. Real Estate Investment Trust (REIT) Market Making: SPV Real Estate Market Making that provides liquidity to REIT markets, enabling investors to buy and sell shares.

4. Blue Water Holding Group real estate investment trust (REIT): SPV Marketing Making with Tokenization and real time bid and offer transaction report.

Conclusion:

Special Purpose Vehicle (SPV) Real Estate Market Making plays a vital role in providing liquidity to real estate markets. By operating through a separate legal entity, SPV Real Estate Market Making can isolate risks, improve efficiency, and promote market transparency. As real estate markets continue to evolve, SPV Real Estate Market Making will remain essential in facilitating the buying and selling of properties.

Know Your Client (KYC)

Know Your Client (KYC) is a critical process in commercial real estate that involves verifying the identity, credibility, and legitimacy of clients, tenants, investors, or partners. The goal of KYC is to prevent fraudulent activities, ensure compliance with regulations, and build trust with clients.

Why is KYC Important?

KYC is essential in commercial real estate for several reasons:

1. Prevents Fraud: KYC helps to prevent fraudulent activities, such as money laundering, identity theft, and terrorist financing.
2. Ensures Compliance: KYC ensures compliance with regulations, such as anti-money laundering (AML) laws and know-your-customer regulations.
3. Builds Trust: KYC helps to build trust with clients by demonstrating a commitment to transparency and accountability.
4. Reduces Risk: KYC reduces the risk of dealing with unscrupulous clients or partners.

KYC Process

The KYC process typically involves the following steps:

1. Client Identification: Verify the client's identity through government-issued ID documents, such as passports, driver's licenses, or national ID cards.
2. Client Verification: Verify the client's address, phone number, and other contact information.
3. Background Check: Conduct a background check on the client to identify any potential red flags, such as a history of fraud or financial crime.
4. Risk Assessment: Assess the client's risk profile based on their business activities, financial history, and other factors.
5. Ongoing Monitoring: Continuously monitor the client's activities and update their risk profile as necessary.

Best Practices for KYC

1. Implement a KYC Policy: Develop a comprehensive KYC policy that outlines the procedures for verifying client identity and assessing risk.
2. Use Reliable Sources: Use reliable sources, such as government databases and credit reporting agencies, to verify client information.

3. Conduct Regular Updates: Conduct regular updates of client information to ensure that it remains accurate and up-to-date.

4. Train Staff: Train staff on KYC procedures and ensure that they understand the importance of verifying client identity and assessing risk.

5. Continuously Monitor: Continuously monitor client activity and update their risk profile as necessary.

Preventing Unethical Business Practices

Unethical business practices can damage a company's reputation, lead to financial losses, and harm stakeholders. Commercial real estate professionals must prioritize ethical behavior and take proactive steps to prevent unethical practices. Here are some strategies to prevent unethical business practices:

I. Establish a Code of Ethics

1. Develop a comprehensive code of ethics that outlines expected behavior and consequences for misconduct.

2. Communicate the code of ethics to all employees, clients, and partners.
3. Ensure that the code of ethics is easily accessible and regularly reviewed.

II. **Foster a Culture of Integrity**

1. Lead by example: Leaders and managers must demonstrate ethical behavior and promote a culture of integrity.
2. Encourage open communication: Create a safe and supportive environment where employees feel comfortable reporting concerns or asking questions.
3. Recognize and reward ethical behavior: Acknowledge and reward employees who demonstrate ethical behavior and promote a culture of integrity.

III. **Implement Robust Compliance Procedures**

1. Establish clear policies and procedures for compliance with laws and regulations.
2. Provide regular training and updates on compliance procedures.
3. Conduct regular audits and monitoring to ensure compliance.

IV. **Monitor and Address Conflicts of Interest**

1. Identify potential conflicts of interest and develop strategies to mitigate them.
2. Establish clear policies and procedures for managing conflicts of interest.
3. Regularly review and update policies and procedures to ensure they remain effective.

V. **Protect Confidential Information**

1. Establish clear policies and procedures for protecting confidential information.
2. Use secure communication channels and data storage systems.
3. Limit access to confidential information to authorized personnel.

VI. **Report Unethical Behavior**

1. Establish a clear reporting process for unethical behavior.
2. Ensure that all reports are investigated promptly and thoroughly.
3. Take appropriate action against individuals who engage in unethical behavior.

By implementing these strategies, commercial real estate professionals can prevent unethical business practices, promote a culture of integrity, and maintain a positive reputation in the industry.

Taxes and Local Government

Introduction

Taxes are an essential source of revenue for local governments, enabling them to provide public goods and services to their citizens. This chapter explores the different types of taxes, how they are collected and allocated, and the role of local government in taxation.

Types of Taxes

1. Property Taxes

Property taxes are levied on real estate properties, such as homes, commercial buildings, and land. The tax rate varies depending on the location, property value, and local government's tax rate.

2. Sales Taxes

Sales taxes are imposed on the sale of goods and services. The tax rate varies depending on the state or local government.

3. Income Taxes

Income taxes are levied on an individual's income or earnings. The tax rate varies depending on the income level and tax bracket.

4. Other Taxes

Other taxes include excise taxes, utility taxes, and hotel taxes.

How Taxes are Collected and Allocated

1. Tax Assessment

Tax assessment involves determining the value of a property or the amount of tax owed. This is typically done by the local government's assessor's office.

1. Tax Collection

Tax collection involves gathering taxes from taxpayers. This can be done through various methods, such as online payments, mail, or in-person payments.

1. Tax Allocation

Tax allocation involves distributing tax revenue to various public goods and services. This can include funding for education, infrastructure, public safety, and healthcare.

Role of Local Government in Taxation

1. Tax Policy

Local governments play a crucial role in setting tax policies, including determining tax rates, exemptions, and deductions.

1. Tax Administration

Local governments are responsible for administering taxes, including tax assessment, collection, and allocation.

1. Tax Revenue Management

Local governments must manage tax revenue effectively to ensure that public goods and services are funded adequately.

Challenges and Opportunities in Taxation

1. Tax Evasion and Avoidance

Tax evasion and avoidance are significant challenges in taxation, resulting in lost revenue for local governments.

1. Tax Reform

Tax reform efforts aim to simplify tax codes, reduce tax rates, and eliminate tax loopholes.

1. Tax Technology

Advances in tax technology, such as e-filing and digital payment systems, have improved tax administration and compliance.

Conclusion

Taxes play a vital role in funding public goods and services provided by local governments. Understanding the different types of taxes, how they are collected and allocated, and the role of local government in taxation is essential for effective tax policy and administration. By addressing challenges and opportunities in taxation, local governments can improve tax revenue management and provide better public services to their citizens.

Respecting Religion in Commercial Real Estate

Respecting religion is an essential aspect of maintaining a positive and inclusive work environment in commercial real estate. Here are some ways to promote religious respect and accommodation:

1. Understand and accommodate religious holidays and practices: Be sensitive to the religious holidays and practices of your clients, tenants, and colleagues. Make accommodations when possible, such as scheduling meetings around religious holidays.

2. Provide prayer rooms and quiet spaces: Consider providing prayer rooms or quiet spaces for clients, tenants, and employees to observe their faith.

3. Respect dietary restrictions: Be mindful of dietary restrictions when hosting meetings, events, or providing food services.

4. Avoid religious bias and stereotyping: Treat all individuals with respect and dignity, regardless of their religious beliefs or practices. Avoid making assumptions or stereotypes based on someone's religion.

5. Foster an inclusive work environment: Promote a culture of inclusivity and respect, where individuals feel comfortable sharing their religious beliefs and practices.

6. Be aware of religious symbols and practices: Be respectful of religious symbols and practices, and avoid displaying or promoting symbols that may be offensive to certain religions.

7. Provide training and education: Offer training and education on religious diversity

and inclusion to promote awareness and understanding.

8. Develop a religious accommodation policy: Establish a policy for accommodating religious practices and beliefs, and ensure that it is communicated to all employees, clients, and tenants.

By promoting respect and understanding of different religions, commercial real estate professionals can create a positive and inclusive work environment that values diversity and promotes success.

"Just Say Nice Words and Thank You" in Real Estate: A Hallmark of Class

In the fast-paced and often competitive world of real estate, it's easy to get caught up in the hustle and bustle of deals and negotiations. However, amidst all the chaos, it's the simple act of saying "nice words and thank you" that can truly set you apart as a professional with class.

Showing Appreciation and Gratitude

A genuine "thank you" or expression of appreciation can go a long way in building relationships and fostering a positive reputation in the industry. Whether it's a client, colleague, or counterpart, acknowledging their efforts and showing gratitude can help to:

- Build trust and rapport
- Strengthen relationships
- Show respect and professionalism
- Create a positive and memorable experience

Demonstrating Class and Sophistication

In real estate, saying "nice words and thank you" is not just about being polite; it's about demonstrating class and sophistication. It shows that you value the people you work with and are committed to building strong, lasting relationships.

Moreover, expressing gratitude and appreciation can help to differentiate you from others in the industry. In a world where everyone is vying for attention and business, a genuine "thank you" can be a powerful tool for standing out from the crowd.

Best Practices for Saying "Nice Words and Thank You"

Here are a few best practices for incorporating "nice words and thank you" into your real estate practice:

- Be genuine and sincere in your expressions of gratitude
- Take the time to write handwritten notes or send personalized emails
- Show appreciation for the little things, not just the big deals
- Make gratitude a habit by incorporating it into your daily routine

Conclusion

In the world of real estate, saying "nice words and thank you" is not just a nicety; it's a necessity. By showing appreciation and gratitude, you can build strong relationships, demonstrate class and sophistication, and differentiate yourself from others in the industry. So, take the time to say "thank you" and watch your business and reputation flourish.

Presentation in Commercial Real Estate: A Key to Success

In commercial real estate, presentation is a critical component of any successful transaction. Whether you're a broker, agent, or investor, presenting properties, reports, and analyses in a clear, concise, and compelling manner can make all the difference in winning clients, closing deals, and achieving your goals.

Why Presentation Matters in Commercial Real Estate

1. First Impressions: A well-crafted presentation can create a lasting first impression, setting the tone for a successful relationship with clients, investors, or partners.

2. Clarity and Understanding: A clear and concise presentation helps to ensure that all parties understand the key points, reducing the risk of miscommunication and errors.

3. Building Trust: A professional presentation demonstrates expertise, attention to detail, and a commitment to excellence, helping to build trust with clients and stakeholders.

4. Competitive Advantage: A well-designed presentation can be a key differentiator in a competitive market, helping to set you apart from others and win business.

Key Elements of an Effective Presentation in Commercial Real Estate

1. Clear and Concise Language: Avoid using jargon or technical terms that may confuse your audience.

2. Visual Aids: Use high-quality images, charts, and graphs to illustrate key points and make the presentation more engaging.

3. Organized and Logical Structure: Ensure that your presentation follows a logical structure, making it easy to follow and understand.

4. Relevant Data and Analysis: Include relevant data, analysis, and market research to support your arguments and demonstrate your expertise.

5. Professional Design and Layout: Use a professional design and layout to make your presentation visually appealing and engaging.

Best Practices for Delivering an Effective Presentation in Commercial Real Estate

1. Know Your Audience: Tailor your presentation to your audience's needs, interests, and level of understanding.

2. Practice and Rehearse: Practice and rehearse your presentation to ensure that you deliver it confidently and smoothly.

3. Use Storytelling Techniques: Use storytelling techniques to make your presentation more engaging and memorable.

4. Encourage Interaction: Encourage interaction and questions from your audience to ensure that they understand the key points and are engaged.

5. Follow Up: Follow up with your audience after the presentation to answer any additional questions and provide further information.

Conclusion

In commercial real estate, presentation is a critical component of any successful transaction. By understanding the importance of presentation, incorporating key elements, and following best practices, you can deliver effective presentations that win clients, close deals, and achieve your goals.

Time Management and Financial Planning for Real Estate Professionals

As a real estate professional, it's essential to prioritize time management and financial planning to achieve success in your career and secure your financial future.

The Importance of Being Timely, Prompt, and Keeping Appointments

In the fast-paced world of real estate, being timely, prompt, and keeping appointments is crucial for building trust and credibility with clients, colleagues, and partners. By being reliable and respectful of others' time, you can:

- Build strong relationships and a positive reputation
- Increase client satisfaction and loyalty
- Stay organized and focused on your goals
- Avoid missed opportunities and lost business

The Importance of Saving for Retirement

As a real estate professional, it's essential to prioritize saving for retirement to ensure a secure financial future. By putting money away in retirement accounts, you can:

- Take advantage of tax benefits and compound interest
- Build a nest egg to support your retirement goals
- Reduce financial stress and anxiety

- Increase your financial independence and flexibility

Retirement Account Options for Real Estate Professionals

As a real estate professional, you have several retirement account options to consider, including:

- SEP-IRA (Simplified Employee Pension Individual Retirement Account)
- Solo 401(k)
- Traditional IRA
- Roth IRA

Consult with a financial advisor or attorney to determine the best retirement account options for your specific needs and goals.

Conclusion

By prioritizing time management and financial planning, real estate professionals can achieve success in their careers and secure their financial future. Remember to be timely, prompt, and keep appointments, and make saving for retirement a priority. With the right strategies and planning, you can build a successful and sustainable real estate career.

Glossary of Key Terms

1. Absorption Rate: The rate at which available space is leased or sold in a given market.
2. Amortization: The process of gradually paying off a debt, such as a mortgage.
3. Appraisal: An independent opinion of the value of a property.
4. Asset Management: The process of managing and maintaining a property to maximize its value and income.
5. Broker: A licensed professional who represents buyers, sellers, landlords, or tenants in commercial real estate transactions.
6. Building Class: A classification system used to describe the quality and age of a building, with Class A being the highest quality and Class C being the lowest.
7. Cap Rate: The rate of return on a property based on its net operating income.
8. Capital Expenditures (Cap-Ex): Expenses incurred to improve or maintain a property, such as renovations or repairs.
9. Cash Flow: The net income from a property after expenses and debt service.

10. Commercial Mortgage-Backed Securities (CMBS): A type of security backed by a pool of commercial mortgages.
11. Commercial Property: A property used for business purposes, such as office buildings, retail centers, and industrial parks.
12. Condominium: A type of ownership where multiple individuals or entities own separate units within a larger property.
13. Contract Rent: The rent agreed upon in a lease agreement.
14. Debt Service: The amount of money required to pay off a loan, including principal and interest.
15. Depreciation: The decrease in value of a property over time due to wear and tear, obsolescence, or other factors.
16. Developer: A company or individual that develops new commercial properties or redevelops existing ones.
17. Due Diligence: The process of researching and verifying the details of a property before making a purchase or investment decision.
18. Effective Rent: The rent paid by a tenant after any concessions or discounts are applied.

19. Escrow: A third-party account that holds funds or documents until certain conditions are met.
20. Eviction: The process of removing a tenant from a property for non-payment of rent or other breaches of the lease agreement.
21. Foreclosure: The process of taking possession of a property due to non-payment of a mortgage or other loan.
22. Gross Lease: A type of lease where the landlord is responsible for paying all expenses, including property taxes, insurance, and maintenance.
23. Gross Rent Multiplier (GRM): A metric used to evaluate the value of a property based on its gross income.
24. Highest and Best Use: The most profitable and feasible use of a property, taking into account its location, zoning, and other factors.
25. Income Approach: A method of valuing a property based on its potential to generate income.
26. Industrial Property: A property used for industrial purposes, such as manufacturing, warehousing, and logistics.

27. Investment Property: A property purchased with the intention of generating income or profits through rental, sale, or other means.
28. Lease: A contract between a landlord and tenant that outlines the terms and conditions of property use.
29. Lease Option: A contract that gives a tenant the option to purchase a property at a predetermined price.
30. Lender: A financial institution or individual that provides financing for commercial real estate transactions.
31. Letter of Intent (LOI): A non-binding document that outlines the terms and conditions of a potential real estate transaction.
32. Market Value: The estimated value of a property based on its highest and best use.
33. Mixed-Use Property: A property that combines multiple uses, such as office, retail, and residential space.
34. Mortgage: A loan secured by a property, used to finance its purchase or development.

35. Multifamily Property: A property used for residential purposes, such as apartments, condominiums, and townhouses.

36. Net Lease: A type of lease where the tenant is responsible for paying all expenses, including property taxes, insurance, and maintenance.

37. Net Operating Income (NOI): The income generated by a property after operating expenses are deducted.

38. Office Building: A property used for office space, such as corporate headquarters, medical offices, and co-working spaces.

39. Operating Expenses: The costs associated with maintaining and operating a property, such as property taxes, insurance, and maintenance.

40. Opportunity Zone: A designated area that offers tax incentives for investments in real estate and businesses.

41. Property Management: The process of overseeing and maintaining a property on behalf of its owner.

42. Property Type: A classification system used to describe the type of property. Such as office.

A Special Thank You!

I would like to extend my sincerest gratitude to you for taking the time to read my book on The Greatest Re-set, Commercial real estate. It is an honor to have been able to share my knowledge and experience with you.

I hope that you found the book informative, engaging, and most importantly, valuable in your pursuit of knowledge and success in the commercial real estate industry. My goal in writing this book was to educate, inspire, and empower you with the insights and expertise needed to navigate the complex and ever-changing world of commercial real estate.

Thank you again for your interest in my book. I am thrilled to have had the opportunity to share my passion and expertise with you. I wish you all the best in your future endeavors and hope that the knowledge and insights gained from my book will serve as a valuable resource for years to come.

Sincerely,
Sheldon Andre

Comments

Christopher Breaux, Board member/ Real Estate Advisor / Director

If you ever considered getting into the world of real estate investing Sheldon Andre's The Greatest Re-set, Commercial Real Estate is a must read. Beneficial for both the experienced and novice alike, the author takes you into a deep dive of what it takes to be successful in this exciting industry. Carefully examining how to navigate through the pitfalls of the market while taking a bare bones approach to proven methods to thrive and prosper. If it's time to get serious about your approach to real estate this book is an essential going forward!

Sarka Ondrackova Bockmeulen, Floral designer/Artist

I never thought I'd be interested in a book about commercial real estate, but Sheldon Andre's 'The Greatest Re-set' is a surprisingly great read for everyone! As a floral designer, I was impressed by the author's ability to break down complex concepts into easy-to-understand language. Whether you're a seasoned investor or just starting out, this book has something for everyone. Sarka Ondrackova Bockmeulen, Floral Designer and Artist.

Calatrava Slade, Chief Editor and Researcher

I've had the pleasure of reviewing Sheldon Andre's latest work, 'The Greatest Re-set: Commercial Real Estate', and I must say, it's a game-changer. Sheldon's meticulous research and insightful analysis provide a comprehensive understanding of the commercial real estate landscape. This book is a must-read for anyone looking to navigate the complexities of the industry. Well done, Sheldon!   Calatrava Slade, Chief Editor and Researcher.

Susana Penalosa, Board member / Advisor

Sheldon Andre's book The Greatest Re-set is a "critical tool" for all interested parties seriously considering investing in real estate. Sheldon's direct approach and careful analysis of today's
real estate landscape is a powerful read for the committed investor..

Sarka Ondrackova Bockmeulen
Artist

Disclaimer and Copyright Notice

Entertainment Purposes Only

The Greatest Re-set, Commercial real estate is intended for entertainment purposes only. The information, opinions, and ideas expressed in this book are not intended to be taken as advice or guidance. Readers should not rely solely on the information presented in this book for making decisions or taking actions.

Copyright Notice

Copyright 2024 / Sheldon Andre. All rights reserved.

No part of this book may be reproduced, stored in a retrieval system, or transmitted in any form or by any means, electronic, mechanical, photocopying, recording, or otherwise, without the prior written permission of the author.

Permission Requests

Requests for permission to reproduce, distribute, or translate any part of this book should be addressed to:

Sheldon Andre
Po Box 752
Canal Point FL 33438

By reading this book, you acknowledge that you have read and understood this disclaimer and copyright notice, and you agree to be bound by their terms.

www.ingramcontent.com/pod-product-compliance
Lightning Source LLC
Chambersburg PA
CBHW071029240526
45469CB00006BD/2148